INSCRIPTIONS

Also by Cammy Thomas

Cathedral of Wish

INSCRIPTIONS

Cammy Thomas

Four Way Books
Tribeca

In memory of Cynthia Sumner O'Neill

Please direct all inquiries to:
Editorial Office
Four Way Books
POB 535, Village Station
New York, NY 10014
www.fourwaybooks.com

Library of Congress Cataloging-in-Publication Data

Thomas, Cammy.
[Poems. Selections]
Inscriptions / Cammy Thomas.
pages cm
Includes bibliographical references.
ISBN 978-1-935536-46-8 (pbk. : alk. paper)
I. Title.
PS3620.H626A6 2014
811'.6--dc23
                              2014011287

This book is manufactured in the United States of America and printed on acid-free paper.

Four Way Books is a not-for-profit literary press. We are grateful for the assistance
we receive from individual donors, public arts agencies, and private foundations.

State of the Arts

NYSCA

This publication is made possible with public funds from the New York State Council on the Arts,
a state agency.

[clmp]

We are a proud member of the Council of Literary Magazines and Presses.

Distributed by University Press of New England
One Court Street, Lebanon, NH 03766

CONTENTS

I. SWEET BROKE DOWN

In the Ruins

No speech can catch
the swing and glide
of our constant war.
Empty fridge, bullet-
pocked driveway;
all the whys
and wherefores flatten
into one black line.

Honestly, love
is a battlefield:
agriculture disappears,
and birds glean the furrows
where we oil
our rusty ploughs.

The Emperor of Oyster Bay

He rode to the hunt with trumpets and guns
in November cold, his voice a drum,
his loyal children dressed in green and gold.

His words rang rifle shots, dogs cowering
behind him, stars rotating as years passed—
and blood wove itself into their cloth,
mutated into shapes of horse and hound
running under him on an icy path.

Air froze as they breathed it, icicles
in the lungs. They were pierced
by that which melted and left no trace.

Current

Though he ordered us not to,
we played a game—

circle the room without touching the floor,
toe to table, heel to chair,

hang above Grandma's Chinese rug
so thick it blinded the weavers,

pink peach blossoms
on a death-black ground.

We crashed and splintered
his precious chairs and tables.

Lit with vodka, he shouted us down,
his charge powering our hearts.

What did we pray as years passed
and the grid of wires shrank to a scorch?

Dress with a Zipper in Front

Though she urged him not to,
every day he pulled her zipper down
spilling her soft flesh in front of her children.

To be fair, the zipper had a large ring
meant for pulling, and he was in love.
Not to pull seemed impossible.

He pulled and waited for her nipples
to wink at him. From the edge of his dark
he reached for her.

And she felt the hair from the back
of his hand at her throat, the hand which—
well no matter, she wanted him that much.

Egypt's Enchanting Queen

A flock of birds
flew with every word he said,
lies like columns of feathers
which fell through the air,
and the birds, cold, aloft,
bore him up and away
beyond the reach of our desolation.

He'd had his moment under the lights,
a teenager at Madison Square Garden,
when he'd rode to victory on
Egypt's Enchanting Queen,
his mother holding the silver
bowl he'd won, his mare
shying away from the photographers.

White birds circled us, their feathers
falling like alphabets into a box
smelling of pipe, bourbon, and wool.

Man and Horse

When he approached she shook
as if doused with ice water,
eyes rolling, mouth working the bit.

He rode sitting back on her kidneys,
using his great weight
to wear her out.

Because she held her neck too high,
he fixed a leather line
from bit to chest,
and pulled her head down.

Dancing sideways under him,
she rubbed against trees and fences,
and every time she bucked him off,
her ears turned toward his gasp.

"Day Binds the Wide Sound"

Two wives holding hands,
together for the only time,
leaning against each other,
old, broken by the wrecking machine—
as his ashes are poured
into the weedy pond.

Soon this sharp fall light
will become deep fog.

"Bitter sound as truth is,"
the water keeps saying,
as the two cry over him,
for the terrible days he didn't come back—
and the terrible days he did.

Frieze

Kitchen of open cans,
basement of mice and mold,
disappeared children,
pheasants running in the woods
far from his silent gun:

now that he's gone, he'll stay
exactly as he was. His voice
will never quaver nor his legs buckle.
He'll glare from his cave,
his eyes searching for whatever moves.

What has the next world designed for him
but a frieze of faces turned away?
I wish I'd never thought of him, but
since I have, his image snaps the trees
and burns in every pool.

Lock

I have the only key
and I keep it on my tongue.

Never unlock, no matter the banging,
the howling on the other side,

no matter whose voice sings
those sad cowboy songs of love.

I like the lock,
the key hot on my tongue.

A letter under the door?
I push it back.

A hank of hair, blonde
and baby-fine? Pushed back.

Only the other me
moves in that world,

the tone-deaf me
who needs no lock or key.

The Other You

The-you-from-then would like the-you-from-now to know
that everything is now, whenever
it happened. Bliss coexists

with the strange creature who ruined us,
and sex is a stop on a road where
terrible beasts expect to be fed.

Our ghosts are always with us,
their stinks, their bad habits, always
as much as we're with them.

Time tries to force you to be just
one. Can you feel the people within,
invisible, but living?

You can't forgive the one who hurt you.
Only the-you-from-then can do that,
and she will never be ready.

Without Talking

I was just asking
            why and
I asked him
            why I couldn't.

He told me to change directions,
            to feel it without talking,

to put aside
            what I live in and for—

like "ventured in the slipstream,"
      like "pair of ragged claws,"
                  like "howlhowlhowlhowl"—

to do it all
            without talking,
without
            my other eyes to warn me.

He said don't use
            what saves you,
your wall, the words

                              (do it without talking),
the words defend
        and don't open—
                    again, again, again,
but they keep…

                            oh and without them

Leak

Heat flows up through cracks in the roof,
melting snow which drips to the steps as ice.

Seams open in the driveway
and streams course down them.

Her eyes won't stay closed—
she blinks to make them tear.

Her eyes tingle and let down,
like breasts full of milk,

seeping, running, good
milk, mild as a green field.

Milk gathers in the gaps
between her ribs.

Please Don't Talk

We're better just embracing
because when you speak
I turn to stone. I can't explain

the way our words have failed us.
I know your will is dedicated, breathless
to do right. I know you think

your words fall well. But what I hear
divides us, your hard-shed tears
like distant waterfalls.

I'm sorry, some gap opened
that isn't filling up again.
I sink into our pillows

as into a satin chamber, calm
but cold. I can't shift toward you.
Please, don't talk.

Her Green Shoes

Her grass-green shoes
pass through our closets,
their tongues broken.

We hover over them,
expecting them to stir,
like stalks in wind.

Our mother wore them
to go dancing,
slender in a pale silk dress,

and wore them
when she went for good—
click click, her heels.

She Had a Lack

...a lack whose blackness she clung to,
its sharp sound held to her ear,

a way of listening for waves
she'd never heard nor was likely to,

an established path of assuming
those coming toward would sail past.

She had sex with her bullish neighbor
in secret, as if it would answer,

would solve the mystery like scotch,
which kept the world always spinning,

as if life were a carnival
rather than something accursed.

The lack bled through—black
dyed her eyes and fell to her lap.

While her children climbed out windows,
walked naked down country roads,

she nursed the lack that always lived
in her kitchen of beautiful burns.

Balm

bath
her sides slipping
divide coalesce

and now she's warm and multitude

our father who art
floating in divinest
our fire
our father
bath

not until the blackened and shriveled thing
that connected her
dropped off

balm

her father's mirror
his eyes set ever deeper
in that oily fire

her heart accessible

her head under

What Was It?

You shrank to one sentence
then lost even that,
gulped air,
chewed nothing.

Was it all sky where you were,
a clear and luminous day,
all dials turned to the right,
full treble and bass?
Were you hearing some symphony
we missed, perceiving only loss?

Did something draw closer
to gather you, your jaw working,
hands quiet in your lap,
the button on your sweater
fastened by a stranger?

Egg

You take us down.

I'll ask a camera
to capture the ruin.

Rupture the egg,
master the sea,

you already have
enough of me.

A Thousand Cuts

Some won't come to your service,
tasting rue.

Remember the twisting knife,

how, blind in his coils,
you made us bleed?

Just tiny cuts,

not dangerous,
made to heal—

like mercy at the end
of every tale.

Sweet Broke Down

My sweet broke down one,
when you died they removed you
without saying goodbye,

but I made them bring your body back
before you were boxed and dropped
in southern New Jersey for final burning.

On East 28th Street they draped a sheet
over your cardboard coffin
and showed us one last time.

No powder and no lipstick—
I was glad they hadn't dressed you up
but let you look pale and gone forever.

We children touched your forehead cold as stone
and saw your hair in spears as if just bathed,
the lines like watercourses on your face,

your crooked mouth slightly open,
a corner of one tooth,
and behind it, black.

Garden of Inexact Forms

An asterisk of earth
is what you are.

You made it for him,
every desalinated well.

You removed the nails,
put clean everything.

You used your eyes,
your hands,

dug his garden
of inexact forms.

Puff of Dust

In the morning, dazed by crowded dreams,
I feel again how glad I am she's dead.
No alarm, no wept regrets, no guilty pleasure
now she's gone. I'm just relieved.
Her face was like a constant speech
I tried to block, her boozy breath
in the assisted living. Every time we asked her,
"Mom, what did you do?" she always answered,
"Nothing." And now, if she's to be believed,
she's nothing greater than a puff of dust.

Here, Bury This

Bury this river of bad
that flows through our kitchen—
tarnishes the silver,
rots the fruit.

And here, bury our letters,
even our love letters,
so many many of them.
Yes dear, yes, of course I love you.

Bury the hospital, bury the doctors,
bury even the thought of them—
deep with us dead for years,
our house a ribbon of wood
vanished into the marsh.

Bury the baby we almost had in the 70s,
then later our dreams of him
staring from across the room.
Yes dear, yes, of course we love you.

Bury all the house contained,
rusted knives on the sideboard,
loaded guns in the gun rack—
bury them, bury them now.

Moth-Eaten Stage

I look out my window at night
and see though black trees
a river of light
where the road should be.

Down the river my father
riding a chestnut mare,
and beside him my aunt
astride with a flask full of gin,

both their faces in flames,
voices breaking the clouds,
and the rest of the night so dark
no stars get in.

They look at the bowl of the world
and they rage at me,
I who can tear them apart
or let them ride.

I in my safe little room
can set them free, or
make them perform forever
on that moth-eaten stage.

II. POEMS IN MEMORY OF
ELEANOR THOMAS ELLIOTT, 1926-2006

1. On the Island of Staffa

I couldn't imagine why you,
so alive then,
were gasping,
almost crying
as we climbed the hill.

Looking over the rocky island,
sliding gulls, whitecaps,
basalt caves booming like timpani,
you pulled a plastic box
from your pocket,
trembling, wrenched it open,
and threw your husband's ashes
into the wind.

Yes, yes, it's dust,
yes it is.
It could be anyone,
and could there be anyone
who wouldn't want this kind of love?

2. Checkmate

I was terrified you'd die while visiting me—
eighty years old, wail in the night,
ambulance racing to forever.

Death was playing chess with us,
like the silhouette man in *The Seventh Seal*
dancing with the scythe.

He wasn't a good player, too distracted,
drifting in and out of the room.
You looked well, moved well—

patent leather shoes, little black dress—
your eyes still could pinion us,
but fear froze my fingers over the pieces.

I sensed checkmate,
didn't want the children to see you after . . .
hoped you wouldn't stay long.

3. Crashed

Shiva, god of creation and destruction,
$\qquad\qquad\qquad$ crashed your skull...

In the deserted tow lot, your car—
$\qquad$ top front sheared cleanly off—

$\qquad\qquad$ and on the collapsed webbed windshield,
$\qquad\qquad\qquad\qquad\qquad$ a pink rosette
$\qquad\qquad\qquad\qquad\qquad$ of blood . . .

We wrench open the crumpled car doors—

$\qquad$ inside,
$\qquad\qquad$ rubber gloves from the medical team,

black patent leather pump,
$\qquad\qquad$ satchels of mail,

$\qquad\qquad\qquad\qquad\qquad$ and between the seats
your small gold watch.

4. Hem of Your Garment

When I last saw you
the garment was a thin sheet,
your face a balloon,
blood still flowing, heart thumping
to the machines.
The blow opened your skull—

just the war of life,
the car, the truck, the soft mystery of the body,
torso untouched under the sheet
still firm and shapely,
fingers on the covers wiped off but bloody.

Jesus gave me water
but I could not kneel to wash you.
Your body went to be burned—
sweet bone we will release you
to that water you love,
that lasting water,
that ash on the mountain.

5. Inscriptions

I inherit rooms
full of the papers you kept,
emptied of their places and persuasions—

souls housed only in photographs:
grandfather in Imperial Chinese robes, 1900,
blooming rhododendrons around the burned house.

I clutch my purpose to me,
purpose which will vaporize traceless.

Time passes—I'm sorry—

someday I will forget you,
your fierce protective love
for me and for so many,
a light for so many.

"Two handfuls of white dust
shut in an urn of brass—"
instant removal, a brutal
truth, a slam, a smear.

6. It Was Enough

If we'd been *your* kids
our clothes would have fit perfectly,
we'd have traveled, and known
the life of Eleanor of Aquitaine.

You felt you didn't do enough—
outings to the stuffed elephants
at the Natural History,
or the bored ones at the Zoo—

not enough to compensate
for your brother's binges
and our mother's hazy martyrdom.

But summers you cut my hair outdoors,
dropping curls into ragged grass,
letting ice melt in your old-fashioned glass.

7. Ring

The ring you always wore,
diamonds and cabochon emerald,
a cold thing
coming to me:

after your accident, I got it back in a hazard bag
bloody from your fingers—
dizzy arcade,
disk whose watery light comes from the wearer.

Someone twisted it off your finger
and gave it to me
in its final hard sweetness.

If I suspend it around my neck,
this metal O, my empty disk
that made it through the wreck,

will your strong grip pull me to you
in that small green stone—
will it drown me?

8. Knell

I can't become you—
my soul is not your soul,
my eyes not your green fire.
My lack, even you can't fill.
Your things summon
your absence.

Your ring gleams on my finger,
its weight vibrating down my spine,
tolling the bell of you,
the knell of you—
I kneel for you
to a strange god who turns—
is it toward us or away?

III. A WINDY KISS, *for Elly*

Recheck

Darling, your doctor,
what did he say
when our visit—
the loop will go where?

May I trace the line
of the last cut on your
torso, sculpted
against black blanket?

Speak to me before—
show it, show your tear,
your bone will go where
with carved idol glaze?

You slide masked
into morphine reek,
sleep like death,
zeroing while we wait.

Hot Spots

Red blockage, bad passage—
matter stuck halfway down.

Without valium she's breathless
from fear—it loosens her tongue

about death's pretty fingers
and delicate hat.

Dust seeps from her eyes,
turns everything grainy.

The doctor eyes the pictures,
says, "Look at the hot spots."

The Covering Sky Is Nothing

Much is the same: arch of sky,
rabbits on the lawn, narrow
animal pathways through the woods.

The other day, standing dizzy
in the garden, she dropped
and curled, unconscious.
Not much between morphine
and the end of everything.

Day by day in the bath, her bones
slowly emerge, show her where she's going.

Hours pass with dog and sleep,
her faithful wife who works and cleans,
dust beams streaming from
the sky so blue it's exactly nothing.

Vines

The vines of pain that
                    twist around
her veins
        and coil their coils,

                    lift their tender tendrils

drawing power
            from impartial gods who

        can't love, just as they
                        can't die.

Drawn to her whispers,
                    her curses,

        do they understand
                        or merely mimic

        her embrace?

Infernal Rose

She dips a sword into herself,
opens the infernal
rose whose thorns lengthen
with tide and flood,
drought and thought. She takes
her flesh gently,
like a surgeon, removes the red
lattices, the walls between her
and what's perfect.

Must I Leave?

Must I leave
this polar world,
my girls
with their glimmering eyes
and airborne souls?

Tick tock
the toys go,
my muddy dress,
my tire chains,
the firepit I made of rocks and stones.

Tick tock—
I feel the enemy
carving me empty
on this blazing plain.

Her Dressing

Every three days they change it to save her.
Day one, the nurse's monitory steps in the hall,
a suck of air as the old bandage comes off.

Day two, she rises to the tepid rooftop pool
overlooking the hospital cranes, as they construct
more sterile rooms for those like her.

Day three, she remembers her friends
have no pain, their food a pleasure,
not a sacrament to appease the leopard.

In dim light she sees translucent
drops of rain on her window—
glass clatters in the fire bus wind.

Sparks

There's a bomb
in the middle
of me—
a bomb in the core
that shakes
like a drum.

There's a bomb
shaped like a heart
in a shadowy cave
in the middle of me,

a bomb that bursts
like lightning
slits a tree,

a bomb
in the middle,
that shakes
like a heart,
that lights
a cave in the middle
of me.

Treatments

Their treatments focus on the hot,
ransacked apartments of her body.

They pump this and wire that,
so even going for a drive
she has to bring a special shot.

Her muscles and tendons
have become a catchment of ruin.

She shuts her nose, her ears,
tries to lift her eyes
beyond the dirty waiting room,

to think of pouring water
filled with silver light, iris husks
rattling in the wind, pure flame.

But no—she's home in bed.

Black sails from the invisible ship
luff at the edge of her horizon,
bring a moment's unconsciousness—

until the painted
hummingbirds whirr her back.

"Think I'll be here next summer?"

We were standing, looking at Cape Cod Bay, the water warm and weedy, no waves to speak of. She curled her toes into hot sand. The cheap umbrella fluttered beside us. A few seagulls, and far away fishing boats hovered at the edges.

Her tiny bathing suit hung on her. She was so thin her tailbone looked more like a tail. Her knees were bigger than her thighs, her hair reddish straw an inch long. Sapphire eyes glared at me from under a white visor.

Brush Me with Honey

When our sun becomes a red giant,
oceans will boil away
and Earth be scorched
and dead forever, so

brush me with honey,
feed me grilled figs,
and we'll swim
in the snapping turtle perfect
water of Walden Pond,
so deep and silky.

Kiss me quickly
in this nacreous solution.

Knock

Her children taste like licorice,
tart and dark, smooth as seals.

She recites their tears,
forming her lips to an ohh or an ayy,

sings their sea voyage,
their fins in the water, pearly horizon.

Something knocks against her teeth,
invisible, irregular, and wet,

as her lips move, tasting death,
tangy as copper.

Consume

She calls herself a rotted log—
but I see a spider
sitting on the couch,
legs drawn up,
guts a knotted mass.

She says she'll stay longer,
do one more experimental trial—
but I see a spider
sitting on the fruit,
mandibles moving.

First the spider was
the disease within her,
then it became her,
it became us—
consume, consume.

Rustle

Body in the fog—tufted
brown grass swept with each breeze—holds
in it your death—you're
so restless—a blind
bag of bones—is
it now?—We all
pray it's now—your
nerves quivering like seeds in wind—dry stalks
of your static breath—white beach
of your flat body hemmed by air—no
talking anymore—and
your eyes stay closed—your
eyes slide under their lids like hands under sheets—face
brown as the rushes and gaunt—hair
a spiked tassel—heart
a spar.

Terminus

I'm on a train, watching
the Atlantic slide by.
Life passes orderly while she
dies—flat shimmer, cormorants dipping,
beaches where swimmers fumble
with their cold suits.

She's got sunlit eyes,
long white body curved,
her sickness in her but not of her.
(The train whistle reminds me of the time.)
Wild marshes, miles of lovely,
indifferent sand.

I sleep, shadows passing
across me like fan blades,
until the rocking stops and the train
exhales its acrid smoke in the terminus.

Last Words

Dreaming and trying to run,
she was in bed, her cold
legs, skin over bone,
trying to stand up and move.

Her mouth a black gap—
none of us slept, watching her sleep—
watching the new world claim her,
its foggy, invisible contours.

The hospice doc put morphine in,
waited, upped the dose, but
still she sighed, finally spoke:
"Is this really it?"

To Mr. D.

I'll say it once:
I'm not leaving.

You can box me in,
but the lights stay on.

I'll cover myself
in hot orange roses.

I'll stay in bed and think of sex
(we liked it when we did it).

I'll kneel, I'll pay—
but I'll keep
my keel.

This knot
of flesh
will stop
your touch.

Conduit

If she's gone, I'm just
a conduit of my gestures.

Nothing explains me but
myself, my hand in the roses.

My laugh chokes
my face in the mirror.

The creaking floor
tells me I'm here.

The thrush sings only from instinct,
not for me, not for her.

I burned and spread her ashes,
a windy kiss the taste of clay.

Ashes

Every time I spread someone's ashes,
they blow back on me,
streak my clothes, sail into my mouth.
They're in me forever—their nightmares,
their fireplaces, their tipsy parties.

Most of the photos on my piano
are of dead people. I see the smoke,
rising from my father's pipe again as he waits
to make a toast at Dorothy's wedding.
And the zipper on that baby's dress
will always be the last thing she felt.

Cheyenne the dog lies forever under
a tree by the pond whose rushes
creep across it as years pass,
and I mow and mow
to keep her memory green and springy
as the grass above her grave.

Hummingbird

No more mornings in bed together,
her cropped blonde hair tinged green
in a bar of sun.

Gone her salty, earthy imprint,
her pile of shells spilling
briny grit into the tub.

No rhythmic swishing
of her toes under the sheet
when she's almost asleep.

Bats skim by the kitchen
where I stand frozen,
holding my spatula.

I see her face
like a hummingbird,
hovering in the window glass.

Chute

After she died, I threw
all the cancer linens down the chute
in the hall of our building.

I slept in those sheets with her
up to the final night, but afterwards,
I couldn't stand the feel of them.

I yanked the bed to face a different wall,
refinished the floor, tossed the drugs
and sharps, gave her clothes away.

She's still here of course.
I talk to her all night—
sometimes she talks back.

Refraction

I go to Walden Pond to convert my solitude. It's dinnertime, sun
low to the water, trees in alpenglow. Believing there are no sharks,
I let my legs dangle. On my back, slightly submerged, I watch the
sun through a few inches of clear water, as it wobbles and spreads
its warm diffused rays—spears of light, flexing saddles of it. Each
bubble reflects the light, vibrating above my face. I'm floating in the
refractions of the sky.

Nothing comes to me. No giant creature opens its jaws on my back.
I'm in the water, every cell cooling, my mind on fire with beauty. It's
not a musical—no children show up to sing about how happy we are,
and the wise old people don't dance on shore to welcome me home.
But cradled by the water I feel the beast retreat. Yes, I'm alone, and
no, that show of light and color is not for me—it merely exists in
implacable nature. Right now I can float in it.

Notes

In "Day Binds the Wide Sound," the quoted lines are from Susan Howe's "Rückenfigur."

The quotations in "Without Talking" are from Van Morrison, T. S. Eliot, and Shakespeare, respectively.

In "Inscriptions," "Two handfuls of white dust, shut in an urn of brass" is a line from Tennyson's "The Lotos-Eaters."

"Hem of Her Garment" takes its title and the line "Jesus gave me water" from traditional spirituals, as performed by Sam Cooke.

"The Covering Sky is Nothing," is a line taken randomly from Shakespeare's *The Winter's Tale*.

The form of "Rustle" was suggested by Jennifer Clarvoe.

Acknowledgments

Thanks to the following magazines for accepting these poems, sometimes in different forms:

Appalachia, Common Ground Review, Eclipse, The Healing Muse, Ibbetson Street Press, The Milo Review, National Trust for Scotland Newsletter, and *Off the Coast.*

I thank, in memoriam, my aunt, Eleanor Elliott; my sister-in-law, Cynthia O'Neill; my mother, Anne M. Thomas; and my stepmother, Susan N. Thomas.

Thanks also to the following people for expert advice over many years: Ramsay Breslin, Jennifer Clarvoe, Julia Lisella, Gail Mazur, Theodora Stratis, Dorothy Q. Thomas, Eleanor Wilner, and Rosamond Zimmermann. I am lucky to be encouraged by my family and friends, especially Augusta, Eleanor, and James Thomas; Claire, Emma, and Tony Siesfeld; Heather and Lorrin O'Neill; Dee Clarke; and Mary McClean. For helping me find time and space, I give thanks to Elizabeth Bedell, Deborah Gray, and Sandy Stott from Concord Academy, to the Ragdale Foundation, and to Elisabeth Sackton and Dennis Balcom. And I owe an ocean of gratitude to everyone at Four Way Books, including Bridget Bell, Victoria McCoy, Ryan Murphy, and especially Martha Rhodes, for helping me in uncountable ways.

Cammy Thomas is the author of *Cathedral of Wish* (Four Way Books), which received the 2006 Norma Farber First Book Award from the Poetry Society of America, selected by Medbh McGuckian. Thomas's poems have recently appeared in *Appalachia, Bateau, The Classical Outlook, The Healing Muse,* and *Ibbetson Street Press.* The recipient of a fellowship from the Ragdale Foundation, she lives in Lexington, Massachusetts, and teaches literature and creative writing at Concord Academy.